D1272321

STARS OVER BETHLEHEM

STARS OVER BETHLEHEM

By *Opal Wheeler*

Decorations by Christine Price

E. P. DUTTON & COMPANY, INC., NEW YORK · 1952

Library of Congress Catalog Card Number: 52-10429

STARS OVER
BETHLEHEM

CHRISTMAS,
that holiest time
of rejoicing, was

usually ushered in each year with a giant snowfall that spun itself into mountainous drifts around our Wisconsin home, keeping us prisoners for days at a time. But rapturous prisoners we were, with the busy hum of festival preparations resounding in every nook and corner of the rambling old house.

11

From morning until nightfall, the delicious smell of popcorn filled the kitchen as young arms sent the iron skillet racing over the red-topped coal stove. Mounds of fluffy kernels were strung for Christmas-tree trimming, stealthily eaten, and needles restrung in a never-ending process.

Whirling paper chains, damp with flour and water paste, trailed through every room. Apples, cranberry garlands, gilded walnuts and stuffed cornucopias were hung and rehung with tireless energy on the un-complaining fir tree. Viewing our homemade decora-tions with critical pride, we sighed with pleasure when not a speck of green branch could be seen through the glittering array.

Twilight calm descended at last, and my joy was complete as I stood at the frosty bay window, watch-ing the endless white rain feathering earthward. In quiet ecstasy I listened to my mother's untrained but

12

infinitely sweet voice caroling through the pearly dusk:

> O little town of Bethlehem!
> How still we see thee lie;
> Above thy deep and dreamless sleep
> The silent stars go by.

From my earliest days of remembering, those simple words of the lovely old song wove a magic scene in the innermost recesses of my being, forever to be sacred and set apart.

My longing to visit that blessed shrine grew to be an obsession that filled even my sleeping hours. In my dreams I flew nightly to little Bethlehem, tucked away in the far-off hills of Judea. Her hallowed streets were washed in silvery starlight, and venturing on noiseless shoes to the very entrance of the manger grotto, my heart was filled with wonder at the glories that I saw there.

13

But in morning sunlight my mother would smile at my rapt expression and, with sympathetic understanding, patted my dark braided head. "Dreams, child, idle dreams," she would say, and go on with her gentle singing of the Bethlehem carol.

There was a peculiar power in that song that brought peace and calm to a household containing seven lively, self-willed children. No matter what the disturbance, the single phrase, "O Holy Child of Bethlehem, descend to us, we pray," was enough to bring instant serenity and contentment.

All of the beloved Christmas carols we knew by heart and sang them with growing enthusiasm throughout the festival season. Each of the exceedingly musical children fashioned fresh harmonies while I accompanied by ear at the old, upright rosewood piano. This was one time of year when I was never hurried off to bed, and in a delirium of joy, played on as long as I wished, after everyone else had found rest under thick winter blankets.

"Silent Night!" "The First Nöel!" "We Three Kings!" The commands from open doorways trailed down to me. Between carols I raced to the black-bellied coal stove, glowing comfortingly in one corner of the snow-lighted sitting room, for spasms of front and back warming.

Each favorite was played, with an ample supply of variations of my own, until all the voices overhead were stilled in sleep. Then, wrapping my long white flannel nightgown about me, I crept, shivering, up the steep back stairs to bed.

But somehow, Christmas Eve was too holy a time for the sound of our own voices, and in the tremulous darkness, the last blessing that we knew was mother's silvery singing of our best-loved Bethlehem carol:

> Yet in thy dark streets shineth
> The everlasting light;
> The hopes and fears of all the years
> Are met in thee tonight.

15

Bethlehem! My longing to visit that little hill town grew with the years and I knew that one day the deepest desire of my heart must be fulfilled.

And so it was, that in an eventful journey encircling the world, the dream of my lifetime was coming true when I found myself, just three short days before the blessed Night of the Nativity, on the way to Bethlehem.

Christmas in the Holy Land! Would it be as I had imagined, all of these long, patiently waiting years? With disquieting emotions of elation and misgiving, I climbed out of the tiny bucket plane that had winged its way through sun-crowned skies from Egypt to Palestine, with a capacity load of four passengers.

Leaving Lydda behind us, we wound by car through the encircling hills in a gentle blue twilight, and with strangely beating heart I soon found myself on the time-worn streets of Jerusalem.

16

Jesus had walked on these very pathways beneath my feet! My desires grew by leaps and bounds. I would wander through His meadows, flowing placidly in every direction beyond the city gates. Down to the Jordan close by I would go to watch the turbulent brown waters cut deeply into the heart of the valley. Following its headstrong way, I would find the bend in the river, hidden by willows and sycamores, where John had given the Christ its blessing.

I would hasten to Nazareth, only a day's journey away, with its flower-scented fields where He had romped as a child. The air was like wine, I was told. And there was the Garden of Gethsemane just over the hill, with a church built over the very rock where He had prayed, anguished, through the lonely silence of the night, beseeching His weary, slumbering Peter and John, "O my disciples, could ye not watch with me one hour?"

17

The ancient olive trees would still be growing in that garden as in the time of the Master, for olive trees extended life by simply putting forth new shoots.

There was the winding, cobbled Via Dolorosa where I would walk, sorrowing, to the fourteen Stations of the Cross and seek the small, white marble sepulcher where He was laid in the vast dead of the night.

All of these things I would do, and many more, with a prayer for so great a privilege spiraling to the serene blue heavens.

But above all, with quickened footsteps I would take my pilgrim way over the triumphant Jerusalem road, out to the well-worn hills and the precious place of His birth, the little town of Bethlehem.

18

THERE WAS

an exhilaration in
the crisp, sun-drenched

air of Jerusalem on the morning before Christmas. In every direction, uphill and downhill, living streams of golden light coursed through her hallowed streets. Her domes and spires and towers, celestial sentinels through the ages, swept startlingly into cloudless blue heavens for closer communion on this blessed day.

21

Only a few short miles away in a little neighboring town among the Judean Hills, the celebration of the greatest event in the lives of men would take place. On the stroke of midnight, the Christmas bells would ring their paeans of exaltation to stir again the pulse of the world.

Bethlehem! The word sang in magical rhythm through the very core of my being. I must get me there quickly to experience soul-stirring moments alone, before eager throngs from all parts of the world would begin their pilgrimages at sundown.

Hastening through the broad, well-cared-for thoroughfares of the new section cresting the hill, I found business thriving in the most modern shops. On side streets, slow-moving venders pushed their grease-stained carts from post to post, ladling sizzling morsels to hungry customers from smoking black kettles, lean dogs waiting mournfully for a stray crumb.

22

At every bend in the road, orange and grapefruit stands were lined with thirsty travelers, drinking brimming glasses of freshly squeezed juices. In few other places on this earth are fruits of such excellence grown as in Palestine.

The strange sight of fair-haired, blue-eyed babies took me by surprise. Never have I seen more beautiful the world over. Lovely as angels they were, basking in the healing sun under the proud, watchful eyes of dark-haired, dark-eyed mothers.

Feeling their way in and out of the crowds on crutch or cane, the poor and aged shuffled to open doorways for their share of copper coins, laid out with loving care on waiting tables.

Everywhere the low, musical *"Shalom"* (peace) passed from lip to lip in friendly greeting.

But the new, modern section did not hold me for long. Down the gentle slopes to the Old City I quickly

wound my way, and once in the steep, twisting cobbled lanes of the ancient, gray-walled center, the glory of the Holy City burst upon me. It was here that the Christ had made His mark for all time.

From afar He had looked down upon Jerusalem. And He had loved this city of contrasts, the heart of the world where East mingled with West, but each carefully preserving through the centuries its own dress and custom and speech, babbling endlessly in sixty different languages.

Time had stood still in this colorful life of an ancient people. The same customs as in the days of the Master were being practiced in the teeming life of the narrow, alley-wide streets. Arabs in long robes, flowing headdress tied on with camel's-hair rope, climbed up and down the wet slippery steps, buying and selling at the rows of stalls in loud, raucous tones.

Meats turned slowly on hand-made spits and yawn-

ing ovens gave a constant supply of freshly baked bread for hungry customers. Hidden away in dark, cavelike shops were precious silks of glowing hue and rugs of rare and ancient design, wonderfully wrought in jewel colors of the rainbow.

In a small open space in the checkered sunlight, merchants bargained in high, whining voices over a few brown, fat-tailed sheep. Near them, peasant women in rough blue costume with faces wrinkled and burned by sun and wind huddled against a stone wall. Solemnly they arranged their trays of nuts and pigeons, olivewood rosaries and miniature vases cut from the stone of the Dead Sea.

With a shock of surprise I came suddenly upon the entrance to the Bethlehem Road. There, towering in massive gray strength before me was the famous Jaffa Gate, called the Gate of the Friend by the Arabs, Abraham, friend of God, having passed here. Stone

25

on gray stone it piled thirty-eight impressive feet above me, welding the tremendous, Turkish-built city walls into a mighty bulwark.

Jesus had walked through this very gate beside the great pile of rock that had once been Herod's palace. He had stood where I was standing now, perhaps looking upon the same strange sights that met my eyes.

Donkeys, camels and goats clattered over the rough cobbles, past heaping pyramids of golden oranges. Now and then they upset a stand of figs and dried fruits hanging on strings from swaying willow poles. From a coffee shop near by, thin trails of smoke told of Syrians drinking tiny cups of the brown syrupy liquid and smoking their hubble-bubble water pipes in deep contentment.

Flat-hatted, black-robed Jews, with prayer rugs thrown about their shoulders, went their quiet way to the place of lamentations to lean their heads against

26

the mellowed stones of the Wailing Wall. The only relics left them after the destruction by the Emperor Titus, they were comforted a little on touching the crumbling ruins as they mourned their sacred Temple, lost to them through the sorrowing ages.

"If I forget thee, O Jerusalem, let my right hand forget her cunning," the favorite psalm found expression on devout lips.

It was hard to leave this fascinating spot, changing and changeless, old and secret, where Mohammedans and Christians and Jews had gathered through the ages, traveling from the ends of the earth to be a part of the life of the Holy City.

What more sacred place to die and be of the chosen few, there in quiet waiting on the slope of the Valley of Jehoshaphat, where Gabriel would blow his trumpet on the day of Resurrection.

Through the narrow close alleyway of Jaffa Gate

I passed, hastily flattening myself against the musty walls to escape the great shoulder-load of stone, bound to the forehead of a panting Sudanese with stout leather thong.

He would have fared better at the gap in the wall a few yards away. One can ride in a carriage through that opening, made for a German emperor at the time of his holy expedition into Syria.

Free of the jostling crowds, I turned onto the tranquil, sun-bathed Bethlehem Road, breathing freely of the crisp, heady air.

Sheer glory spread around me in the blessed Judean Hills, bubbling in every direction, rising and falling and rolling away to far horizons, the edges melting softly in amethyst haze. The peace of the ages was here, and the spirit of a Presence hovering over the time-worn hills communicated itself to me in purest exultation.

28

The scene before me was unchanged from Bible days. On this very roadway, under the blessing of the skies, the Master had walked and talked with His faithful ones, unfolding the miracles of the spirit in the peace and beauty of the ancient hills.

At that moment the quiet was broken with an eerie call threading from a slender white minaret soaring into the blue behind me. I turned quickly to listen enchanted to the quavering voice of the muezzin, high in his watch tower, calling the Moslems to prayer.

This delicate little gleaming finger was part of the startling and majestic beauty of Jerusalem. Her many temples were crowned with the crescent, the cross, or the star, etched cleanly against cloudless heavens.

Jerusalem, City of Peace! How often she had strayed from the true meaning of her name. A city set upon a hill, she was still the victor enthroned, a proud eagle on her aerie of pink rock, buffeted by timeless

winds from desert and sea. A miracle citadel through the ages, she stood there indestructible, with heart throb vibrant and steady after destruction and endless degradation through her darkened past had bowed her anguished head to the will of the conqueror.

Bethlehem was waiting for me, five miles away over the beckoning hills. I would walk every foot of the winding ribboned pathway, better to dream of the days that had been.

Israelites and Philistines, Egyptians and Babylonians, Romans, Crusaders and Emperors had marched here in proud array. Abraham, the Nomad, had shepherded his sheep on these grassy slopes on his way to Hebron, pitching his goatskin tent under the kindly protection of the heavens for hours of well-earned rest.

30

But above all, and my pulse quickened at the thought, Mary and Joseph had journeyed here on their way to the City of David for census enrollment in the days of Caesar Augustus.

And because December can be a very stormy month in the Holy Land, with lashing sleet and rain and even snow, it may have been cold among the brown hills. It had taken long days to come from their home in Galilee and perhaps even now Joseph was urging the weary donkey onward with its precious burden to reach Bethlehem before nightfall, lest the guards turn them away at the city gates.

Up a steep hill they would be climbing now, Joseph comforting Mary, heavy with child, and hoping in his heart for a comfortable, safe place for her on this night of all nights. A gnawing hunger possessed her,

but the supply of food was all too low, and stopping by the wayside where a field of peas was in pod, Joseph begged for a handful to satisfy her desire.

The legend story goes on. In hasty refusal the farmer answered and the curse had descended speedily. In the twinkling of an eye, the field of peas was turned to small round stones. To this day the ground is covered with them, a plague to the tiller of the soil with his handmade plow.

There, just ahead on the left of the roadside was a curious landmark, an ancient white circular headstone of a well, with a great hole cut in its center. And Mary must have drunk deeply of its waters and been refreshed. It was soon to bring its blessing to the Three Wise Men as well, for they had lost sight of the guiding star behind them in Jerusalem.

Weary and disheartened, they had stopped by the well to consider, and bending their anxious heads to

drink, saw there the radiant star reflected brightly in its waters. Since that night, the curious landmark has been called the Magi's Well.

The top of the hill and Mâr Elyâs at last, where Mary must surely have rested. And if she were not too weary, what heavenly vistas her eyes must have feasted upon; such grandeur as to have given her fresh courage for the last lap of her journey.

Now she could see two cities, Jerusalem soaring into the heavens behind her, and ahead, blessed little Bethlehem atop its crescent-shaped hill. Far down the eastern valleys glittered long azure stretches of the Dead Sea, and there, climbing gently, were the mountains of Moab in soft purple garments.

The roadway was becoming more traveled now, and pilgrims passing by stopped at Rachel's Tomb, covered with a Moorish dome on the right, to lament or pray in memory of the sorrowing mother who

mourned her life away for her precious little ones.

Long camel trains, their nodding heads fastened to leathern string, undulated over the sparse land as they went their sober way across the valley. And there, clopping in heavy sandals along the highway was a little housewife of Bethlehem, returning from marketing in Jerusalem. Now and then she wrapped her shawl more closely around some object under her arm. At my questioning look, she carefully uncovered the head of her pet chicken, and to my astonished ears, said laughingly in broken English, "My hen like to go with me to market!"

Before me stretched the plains where the young David had roamed with his trusty sling. And the dark-eyed, spirited Bedouin boys were using the same weapon to advantage to this day. What a merry, care-free lot they were, with impish black heads wound in variegated wrappings like their fathers. Their multi-

colored garments, as in the time of Joseph, flowed behind them as they raced over the fields on muscle-hardened legs, healthy lungs exercised by rousing cries.

For all their mischief-making, their keen eyes were ever on the alert. Whenever a lamb or goat strayed too far afield, out came the handmade sling, and the stone, rarely missing its mark, brought the culprit flying back to join its brothers.

Large bands of Bedouin tribes still roamed the country, living in tents at night, and with the dawn, moving on to new pasture lands with their donkeys, camels and goats.

There, just before me, was Bethlehem! I had arrived at last at the place of my longing. Called Beit Lahm in the Arab tongue, it meant simply the House of Bread. There it stood, that blessed little town on its hilltop surrounded by fertile fields and orchards

35

and plains. Its white, flat-topped houses were huddled closely together in the center, the heavy walls of the Church of the Nativity looming grayly on the left.

Silhouetted against the glory of the blue sky, and crowning one corner of the sanctuary, was the low open turret housing the famous Christmas bells that would ring round the world this night in celebration of the birthday of a little Child.

Up the steep, carefully terraced slope of the hill I climbed, each little patch of ground on either side of the roadway separated from its neighbor as in Bible times, and planted with fig and olive orchards.

At the top of the ridge and along a little pathway was the old well that David had known as a boy. And when in later years he was in hiding in the Cave of Adullam, surrounded on all sides by fierce enemies, he longed for a drink of the water whose sweetness he had known so well.

36

Three of his mightiest warriors offered to brave the dangers to satisfy his desire, and in the darkness of night accomplished their mission for love of their leader. But when David held in his hands the sparkling liquid, he could not drink, but poured it on the ground, instead, declaring that it now signified the precious blood of the three who had so willingly risked their lives to do his bidding.

The curving roadway wound sharply into the Bethlehem streets, very narrow and deeply-rutted in places, house walls rising abruptly and shutting out the light of the sun.

Everywhere there were busy Arabs, the men with bulging orange turbans or red tarbush on their heads. The liquid-eyed women might have stepped from the Middle Ages with their high white headdresses falling over their shoulders and down the backs of red embroidered jackets and blue skirts.

Through the crowded passageways they took themselves quietly and with simple dignity, their babies astride one shoulder while they marketed at the well-supplied stalls lining the streets.

The whirr of cutting and polishing wheels sounded through open doorways as skilled workmen bent over their mother-of-pearl rosaries and beads and boxes, the art taught originally to a few inhabitants of the town by monks of the sixteenth century.

On side streets orderly little places of business supplied cities as far away as Damascus with curios of every description. Clean as could be were the small shops, keepers busily whisking every trace of dust from the heavily laden shelves and wares spread under glass.

One quiet-spoken Arab came to his doorway to welcome me in excellent English, explaining that all was in readiness for Christmas customers. When I exclaimed over the beautifully embroidered jackets and

38

blouses and caps, he told me with pride of the many patient months it had taken to fashion them, all wrought with great care by industrious Bethlehem women, long famed for their needlework.

And a very hard life these women led, beginning with early marriage. Still using age-old implements in their simple homes, they toiled unceasingly from sunup until dark, but always with a sense of satisfaction in seeing their families well cared for. And above all is their strong pride in being a part of the consecrated town of Bethlehem.

Through the famous stone courtyard in the center of the town I followed a little girl mother, watching the loving care with which she held her first-born. A wobbly little bundle it was, one tiny leg dangling over her breast, the other down her back.

She smiled at me with gentle dignity, her eyes tender and uncomplaining under her snowy headdress which, with her dowry of gold and silver coins

39

dangling from a stiff board across her forehead, must have weighed from five to eight pounds. But even at night she refused to part with her crowning glory, complaining of headache if for any reason it was taken from her.

The little mother was taking her baby to the manger of the Christ Child for the greatest blessing that it would ever know. I stepped back hastily and found that I was at the very doorway of the Church of the Nativity! What a fortress-like structure it was, built as a protection not only over the manger grotto, but housing under its roof two churches, underground caves, and several monasteries, as well.

The low doorway, cut into the deep stone, kept marauders and stray animals from wandering into the sacred portals. And many times in the past there had been sore need of protection from the enemy hordes that had swept down upon her.

40

There were the Persians who, setting out to sack and burn all places of worship throughout Palestine, strode in mighty conquest to the very doors of the Church of the Nativity. Bent on complete destruction, they were about to begin their deadly work when, looking at the colorful scenes laid in fine mosaic above the doorway, they saw themselves pictured there. The Three Wise Men in Persian dress were on bended knee before the Christ Child, offering their gifts of gold and frankincense and myrrh. With one accord the warriors entered the church and worshiped there also.

With a feeling of exultation I bent my head to enter the low doorway and found myself in the dim and misty Church of Constantine, a forest of gigantic brown stone pillars separating the aisles. To these very colmuns, with traces of Bible scenes still discernible on their smooth surfaces, horses had been

41

tied when the church was made into a stable under the conquering reign of the Turks.

As I stood there, a spectral voice from the shadows bade me look down through the open trap doors in the floor and there, three feet below, in intricate stone mosaic, were pieces of the original flooring laid at Justinian's command three hundred years after the Child was born. I was standing in the oldest Christian church in use today.

My footsteps echoed through the dusky aisles of the vast, beautifully proportioned sanctuary, so simple with whitewashed walls and great hooded lamps hanging from the beamed ceiling. Through the opening at the end I found myself at the top of a steep flight of stairs cut into the rock that led to the manger grotto where the Christ Child was born.

With bated breath I clung to the slender railing and in the semidarkness descended slowly the time-worn steps to the low cave room. There, in the dim,

flickering light from fourteen silver lamps, hanging from the roof of the grotto, I fell to my knees before the silver star set into the marble floor marking the place where the Child had been born. The simple Latin words followed the points of the star:

HIC DE VIRGINE MARIA JESUS CHRISTUS NATUS EST.

As I knelt there alone, my heart overwhelmed in this holiest place on earth, the silence was broken by the sound of childish voices and merry tripping footsteps above me. And there, hopping down the steps was a host of little girls. Dressed in blue, with white pinafores, shoulder pieces bobbing as they descended, they were for all the world like a flock of bright angels.

In an instant they were on the floor, scrambling to kiss the star, and the next moment were on their knees in little blue rows. Two white-clad women led them in their prayers and their responses were amazingly

43

quick and alert. All but one small angel, Sheila, who was busily collecting the lighted tapers left by devout pilgrims, until apprehended by her shocked elders and hastily put into prayerful line.

Their devotions finished, the little ones turned to the manger altar a few feet away and, with ecstatic exclamations, extended their arms to a waxen figure of the Christ Child lying on a miniature bed of straw. The small body was wrapped in swaddling clothes, as is still the custom of newborn Bethlehem babies to this day, tiny bones encouraged to grow straight with the tightly wound band.

My eyes had grown accustomed to the light of the ever-burning lamps that cast a reddish glow on the rich silver and gold tapestries lining the walls. How I longed for the bare rock, instead! At an intersection, I cautiously pushed aside the heavy stiff material and, in great joy, found the rough gray stone beneath my hand.

No room in the inn! I thought of that simple dwell-

ing erected over this natural cave in the rock, as is even now the custom in Palestine building. No doubt but that one side of the stable was open to the weather, a food trough for the beasts at its edge.

The muleteers would have found little difficulty in sleeping in the dark corners with the heat of the animals to keep them warm. But Mary and Joseph, unused to such hardship, would have found little rest, waiting anxiously on their beds of straw.

The caves stretched on, six in all, dim lights showing the musty passageways connecting them. Next to the manger grotto, in a damp rock cell, the good St. Jerome had closeted himself in peace for many patient years, with only a faint light coming from an opening high in the wall to help him in his gigantic task of translating the Bible into Latin.

Through these very rocky caverns, Mary and Joseph had fled with the Child into Egypt to escape the wrath of Herod, who feared the infant claimant to his throne. But twenty fair baby boys, brought to the

caves for safety, paid with their lives that first Christmas, massacred at the cruel command of the infamous leader.

The sound of pure singing above me startled me from my thoughts. Because the grotto was no longer mine, with a steady stream of visitors making constant entrance, I climbed the steep steps opposite and found in the modern Church of St. Catharine a group of kneeling Bethlehem women, their headdresses shining whitely through the dusky aisles. The ardent worshipers might have been young Marys, so exalted was their song and full toned, coming from their hearts in reverent love for a little Child, whose birthday they had already begun to celebrate.

The last red sunrays were leaving Bethlehem with parting blessing and night preparations had begun in earnest. Mothers were rounding up their little ones and herding them indoors for vegetable stew and flat cakes of unleavened bread.

46

Merchants, weary with trading in Jerusalem, urged their camels and donkeys through the narrow lanes with throaty command. Peasant women and children with great armloads of firewood on their heads, loosed them at their doorways, their day's work at an end.

The great square before the Church of the Nativity was alive with pilgrims arriving every moment by car, bus, on horse or muleback and some on foot. Lines of stalls had been hastily erected around the edges of the court and were already serving hungry wayfarers from steaming kettles and with strings of dark sizzling meats and row after row of bright-colored drinks.

The light had already begun to leave the skies, and feeling my way through the jostling crowds, I went down through the valley toward the Field of the Shepherds, a long stretch of rising ground, muted in winter dress. How peaceful were the pasture lands in the first gentleness of evening, the approaches dotted with al-

mond, apricot and peach trees, olive and fig orchards.
Here and there slender cypresses lifted their black
crosses into the tremulous sky.

On these plains, rising and falling in soft brown
harmony, David the shepherd boy had tended his
sheep, practicing songs to soothe the troubled mind
of the king. A beautiful lad he must have been, this
slender, fair-haired youth who was one day to become
lord and master himself and rule proudly as king
over the lands around Bethlehem, to be called David's
City, after him.

My feet were treading the stubble fields now, to
find little patches here and there wrinkled and fur-
rowed with plowing. On these very plains, so long
ago on a wintry night, shepherds had tended their
flocks, all unknowing of the glory that was soon to
shine around them.

One lonely star in the green of the sky glowed

48

softly, and the beautiful story, told so simply by St. Luke, swept into my mind.

And there were in the same country shepherds abiding in the field, keeping watch over their flock by night. And lo, the angel of the Lord came upon them, and the glory of the Lord shone round about them; and they were sore afraid. And the angel said unto them, Fear not: for, behold, I bring you good tidings of great joy, which shall be to all people. For unto you is born this day in the city of David a Saviour, which is Christ the Lord. And this shall be a sign unto you; Ye shall find the Babe wrapped in swaddling clothes, lying in a manger. And suddenly there was with the angel a multitude of the heavenly host praising God, and saying, Glory to God in the highest, and on earth peace, good will toward men.

There on the field was the rocky cave that had given shelter to the simple tenders of sheep on the night when the angel appeared to them. And bending and twisting its gnarled body, the better to see the stars, was the ancient olive tree whose branches had

49

shielded the quaking shepherds from the blinding light of the heavens.

Suddenly, threading over the blessed field in the half darkness came an old melody, the shepherd's song. A small band of singers loomed from the shadows, caroling under the first stars their meaningful song to the vast dome above.

> While shepherds watched their flocks by night,
> All seated on the ground,
> The angel of the Lord came down,
> And glory shone around.

The heavens were hung thickly now with glowing lamps, radiating jewels in a sea of misty blue. Surely at any moment the Wise Men on their straggly camels

would steal from the darkness and go lumbering across the Field of Boaz, nearer the end of their journey than they knew.

But what was that exquisite sound that would usher them into the city? The infinitely tender "Silent Night, Holy Night" stole over the plains in tones of such purity as to dim my eyes with its sheer beauty. Anything so holy must soar aloft to the very skies, enough to bring the angels a little nearer the earth in wondering listening.

> Silent night, holy night,
> All is calm, all is bright,
> Round yon virgin, mother, and Child.
> Holy Infant, so tender and mild,
> Sleep in heavenly peace,
> Sleep in heavenly peace.

I followed the singer and his chorus back toward the city, the faithful stars lighting the way. The low white buildings of little Bethlehem, resting patiently on crescent hilltop, glowed cleanly, one by one, under the watchful heavens.

As we neared her hallowed streets, the urging of our spirits found release in the timeless words of Phillips Brooks:

> O little town of Bethlehem!
> How still we see thee lie;
> Above thy deep and dreamless sleep
> The silent stars go by.

When we reached the square, it was to find milling crowds clamoring entrance to the Church of St. Catharine for the midnight services. My precious permission was checked minutely by the guards and I was allowed to pass through the sacred portals.

Then began the endless climbing of stairs, and by

devious routes and past monastery dwellings, I arrived at last at the very roof top of the church, to find a small group waiting there. But the little-used door resisted all our efforts and we sat in silent waiting on our high watch tower.

Nine strokes of a solemn bell rang through the frosty air, intoning the hour. What glory to commune with the brooding night, a little nearer the radiant heavens. The trembling stars seemed just overhead, pausing over this holy place before moving on in their endless course to eternity.

The spell of the night was broken by a cheery, black-robed brother who had at last found the enormous key. With some difficulty he unlocked the creaking door and ushered us with quiet dignity to the narrow overhanging balcony of the church.

What a change from the dusky aisles of the worshiping Bethlehem mothers! Thousands of candles

glowed on the altar and the great lamps were lighted, revealing an immense throng that overflowed into every inch of space below.

From all parts of the world these prayerful souls had come, many in strange and curious dress, to pour out their thanks for the greatest gift to mankind. Rich and poor alike were gathered there, the great and the lowly in simple humility.

The services began with a flood of music from the organ that swept with majesty and power over the wondering audience. The orchestra and a chorus of trained singers raised their voices in exultant te deums as two hundred dignitaries from near and far conducted the services in rich vestments of gold and crimson and lace, magnificent to behold.

Precious incense floated gently through the church from swinging golden censers. The intoning of the services went on ceaselessly for full five hours in ecstatic devotion, enriched with glorious flights of music, now pure and ethereal from young boy sopranos, now rich and full with male chorus and organ and violins.

No room in the inn! My thoughts sped to the little cave far below, the rude shelter where Mary had rested uneasily on her bed of straw, the faithful Joseph near at hand to give her comfort.

Suddenly a baby's low cry had pierced the gloom of that manger stall, a clear call that was forever to bring peace and comfort to the hearts of men.

Midnight struck the hour and the giant star over

the altar burst into flame, proclaiming the birth of a little Child. The clangor of the Christmas bells overhead pealed round the world with deafening din while exultant Hallelujahs rang from the chorus: "He is born! Glory to God in the highest!"

Up, up to the rafters and on into the starry night swept the glad tidings. In that wondrous and awe-inspiring moment, the audience fell to its knees in exalted prayer. And below, in the manger, two brothers kept silent watch. Three more hours of hosannahs rang without ceasing and at last, when the services were ended, a processional, led by the dignitaries, formed round the church to begin the sacred pilgrimage to the manger grotto.

OUT ON THE

roadway in the clear

frosty morning, I

looked back at hallowed little Bethlehem, glowing softly in the fading starlight.

Its mission was again fulfilled. Once more its ageless bells had rung round the world their message that peace would still the anxious hearts of men, and the warm comfort of good will bind them more closely together, one to another, on this cherished earth of ours.

59

THE
END